D1716139

Hilarious Hedgehogs

Kelly Doudna
AUTHOR

C.A. Nobens
ILLUSTRATOR

Consulting Editor, Diane Craig, M.A./Reading Specialist

A Division of ABDO
ABDO
Publishing Company

visit us at www.abdopublishing.com

Published by ABDO Publishing Company, a division of ABDO, P.O. Box 398166, Minneapolis, Minnesota 55439. Copyright © 2013 by Abdo Consulting Group, Inc. International copyrights reserved in all countries. No part of this book may be reproduced in any form without written permission from the publisher. SandCastle™ is a trademark and logo of ABDO Publishing Company.

Printed in the United States of America, North Mankato, Minnesota
102012
012013

Editor: Liz Salzmann
Content Developer: Nancy Tuminelly
Cover and Interior Design and Production: Kelly Doudna, Mighty Media, Inc.
Photo Credits: Ross Heywood, Fotolia (Alexey Khromushin, kinah2), Shutterstock

Library of Congress Cataloging-in-Publication Data

Doudna, Kelly, 1963-
  Hilarious hedgehogs / by Kelly Doudna ; illustrator C.A. Nobens.
     p. cm. -- (Unusual pets)
  ISBN 978-1-61783-399-1
  1. Hedgehogs as pets--Juvenile literature. I. Nobens, C. A. ill. II. Title.
  SF459.H43D68 2013
  599.33'2--dc23
                            2011050726

SandCastle™ Level: Transitional

SandCastle™ books are created by a team of professional educators, reading specialists, and content developers around five essential components—phonemic awareness, phonics, vocabulary, text comprehension, and fluency—to assist young readers as they develop reading skills and strategies and increase their general knowledge. All books are written, reviewed, and leveled for guided reading, early reading intervention, and Accelerated Reader® programs for use in shared, guided, and independent reading and writing activities to support a balanced approach to literacy instruction. The SandCastle™ series has four levels that correspond to early literacy development. The levels are provided to help teachers and parents select appropriate books for young readers.

Emerging Readers
(no flags)

Beginning Readers
(1 flag)

Transitional Readers
(2 flags)

Fluent Readers
(3 flags)

Contents

Unusual Pets

Unusual pets can be interesting and fun! Unusual pets might also eat unusual food. They might have special care needs. It is a good idea to learn about your new friend before bringing it home.

There are special laws for many unusual animals. Make sure the kind of pet you want is allowed in your city and state.

Hedgehog Basics

Type of animal

Hedgehogs are **mammals**.

Adult size

6 to 30 ounces (170 to 850 g)

Life expectancy

3 to 10 years

Natural habitat

deserts, forests,
and **grasslands**

Kevin has a pet hedgehog.
He holds it gently.

Jennifer wears gloves when she pets her hedgehog. Its **quills** are sharp.

Hedgehogs love to eat fruit and insects. Erin gives her hedgehog an apple as a treat.

Hedgehogs often get along with other pets. John's cat and hedgehog **snuggle** together.

A Hedgehog Story

Spike the nervous hedgehog
decides to roam around.
He sneaks out of his pen.
He leaves without a sound.

He steps onto the path
where orange and red leaves fall.
The moving shadows scare him.
He rolls into a ball.

Spike tiptoes down the path.

He wonders at all he sees.

A soft sound startles him.

It's a caterpillar's **sneeze**.

He hears another noise.

It's just an earthworm's **cough**.

Spike takes a slow, deep breath.

He once again sets off.

Spike listens to the plops
of brown acorns dropping.
He looks behind the tree.
He sees a happy rabbit hopping.

Next to the path is a rock.
Spike thinks he hears it talking.
It's just two chatty grasshoppers.
Spike nods and keeps on walking.

Spike comes up to a **puddle**
and has an awful fright.
A face stares right back at him.
It has eyes as dark as night.

Spike takes a second look.
He breathes a tiny sigh.
It's just his own reflection.
He waves and says good-bye!

Fun Facts

* Pet hedgehogs come in many different colors. Some of the colors are salt and pepper, cinnamon, and apricot.

* The average hedgehog has more than 5,000 **quills**. The quills are hollow inside.

* Many hedgehogs enjoy playing with empty toilet paper rolls. This activity is so common that it has its own name. It's called "tubing."

Hedgehog Quiz

Read each sentence below. Then decide whether it is true or false!

1. A hedgehog's quills are sharp.

2. Hedgehogs don't like to eat fruit.

3. John's hedgehog **snuggles** with his dog.

4. Spike sees a happy rabbit.

5. Spike sees his reflection in a **puddle**.

Glossary

cough – the act or sound of suddenly forcing air out of your lungs.

grassland – a large area of land covered with grasses.

mammal – a warm-blooded animal that has hair and whose females produce milk to feed their young.

puddle – a small pool of water or other liquid.

quill – one of the sharp, hollow spines on a porcupine or hedgehog.

sneeze – the act or sound of suddenly forcing air out through your nose or mouth.

snuggle – to curl up with or lie close to.